Montana Wildflowers

A beginner's field guide to the state's most common flowers

For Claire
Ben, Danny, and Anja

With love,
DD & Bevy

Interpreting the Great Outdoors

Nature's wonders, such as the wildflowers, are certainly remarkable, but unfortunately many people—especially young people—know little about them. That's one reason Falcon® has launched this series of books called Interpreting the Great Outdoors.

Other books in the series include *The Tree Giants: The Story of the Redwoods, the World's Largest Trees; The Fire Mountains: The Story of the Cascade Volcanoes; Montana Wildlife; Where Dinosaurs Still Rule; California Wildflowers; Arizona Wildflowers; Oregon Wildflowers; Minnesota Wildflowers; Montana Wildflowers; North Carolina Wildflowers; and Texas Wildflowers.*

To get extra copies of this book or others in the series, please visit your local bookstore, or write to Falcon, P.O. Box 1718, Helena, MT 59624. Or call toll-free 1-800-582-2665. Falcon® publishes and distributes a wide variety of books and calendars, so be sure to ask for our free catalog, or visit our website at www.falconguide.com.

Botanical consultant: Jan Nixon, Montana Native Plant Society
On the front cover: bitterroot (the state flower), huckleberry, glacier lily, Indian paintbrush, and camas.

Design, editing, typesetting, and other prepress work by Falcon®
Helena, Montana. Printed in Hong Kong.

Library of Congress Number 91-58054
ISBN 1-56044-118-6

Contents

Introduction

Zing! The brilliant yellow and deep red colors of a wildflower grab your attention. On bent knee to look more closely, you can sniff the lovely fragrance and admire the beauty. While there, it's easy to notice more flowers, tiny and shy, tucked close to the earth. Shiny green leaves have many shapes and sizes, and the world of flowering plants becomes more interesting. Some plants are just poking up through the ground. Others have tightly furled buds not yet ready to open. Still others are in full bloom.

Flowering plants have existed for about 120 million years. They started evolving when dinosaurs roamed the earth. Flowers are unique because each seed has a protective, nourishing shell that helps the seed survive.

The sweet nectar of wildflowers entices nectar-drinkers that pollinate the blossoms. The pollinated blossoms then produce seeds. A nice trade! So when you see a bee or an ant crawling inside a flower or watch a hummingbird or butterfly sip nectar, remember they are essential to the survival of flowers. In addition to providing food, flowers may provide shelter for insects and other little creatures.

Montana has about 2,500 species of flowering plants. Different wildflowers have learned to live in the different habitats found in the state, including high mountains, shady forests, and dry prairies.

Flowers have common names, like our nicknames, that often tell something about them. Shooting star, fairy slipper, or elephant head are descriptive names. But these names can be confusing because many flowers have several common names. If you get confused, try learning the scientific names. They are often descriptive, too, but they are in Latin instead of English. The scientific name of each flower appears next to the flower's picture.

Lie on your back and look at a flower as it splashes color up to the sky. Turn onto your side and get an ant's-eye view of the world. Then go belly-down to see how many different plants are growing right under your nose. It's amazing!

Pinwheels of sparkling snowflakes
And soft prisms in raindrops
Snuggle into the Montana soil
—giggling—
Waiting to re-emerge
As the rainbow of colors
Adorning wild flowers

Subalpine Regions

Montana's subalpine wildflowers live a hard life. In the mountains where they live below timberline, snow piles up all winter. Then in summer it melts and gushes through the fields and forests. The wind can blow really hard, and just when you think it's finally summer, it might snow again.

Many wildflowers here grow close to the ground for protection from the strong winds and intense storms. Most are perennials that have learned to flower and produce seeds quickly in the short growing season. Here you can find brilliant blossoms with some of the sweetest fragrances in the world. June and July are usually the best months to see subalpine wildflowers.

Wander through the open parks and stands of subalpine fir and Engelmann spruce trees. Watch for mountain goats or playful Clark's nutcrackers and gray jays. Enjoy this top-row seat for viewing sunsets. Listen to the snowmelt trickle down the mountain.

Cushion Phlox

other names: none
height: 2 to 6 inches
season: April to June

The sweet scent of phlox is especially fragrant at sunset. The blossom's narrow tube invites butterflies and other long-tongued flying insects to sample the nectar, but the sticky stem discourages crawling insects such as ants. The flowers can be pink, white, or blue.

Phlox pulvinata

Alpine Forget-Me-Not

other names: none
height: 1 to 4 inches
season: June to August

Who could ever forget this tiny blossom's perfect blue petals surrounding a miniature yellow sun? The small, furry leaves snuggle close to the ground to find protection from cold mountain winds. Interesting tales surround the forget-me-not—tales of sweethearts, whispered secrets, and treasure caves.

Eritrichium nanum

Heather

other names: Mountain Heath
height: 2 to 12 inches
season: July to August

Few sights are prettier than a patch of heather in bloom. You might expect to hear a tinkling wind-chime sound from the perfect little pink, bell-shaped flowers. The woody stem of the heather is often a showy red, and the leaves look like pine needles. In autumn, look for tiny gold dots on the dark red seed capsules.

Phyllodoce empetriformis

Moss Campion

other names: Cushion Pink
height: only 0.5 to 1 inch, but often a foot or more across
season: June to August

This isn't a true moss, but it looks something like one with its narrow, needlelike leaves. The moss campion doesn't bloom until it's ten years old. It might reach a foot in diameter by the age of twenty-five. Maybe this is what's meant by a "late bloomer!" This plant has a sturdy taproot to help hold it in place at the summit of a windy, treeless peak.

Silene acaulis

Explorer's Gentian

other names: Mountain Gentian
height: 2 to 12 inches
season: July to October

These remarkably blue, funnel-shaped blossoms close at night or when it rains to help the plant protect its pollen from water damage. Indians and settlers used the gentian root to make a tea to treat indigestion and other ailments.

Gentiana calycosa

Yellow Stonecrop

other names: Orpine
height: 4 to 8 inches
season: July to August

If stones could blossom, this would surely be their flower. Look for these yellow, star-shaped flowers on dry, stony mountain slopes. The waxy leaves are succulent and help the plant survive hot, dry summers. *Sedum* is Latin for "sit." Notice how the stonecrop sits close to the ground.

Sedum stenopetalum

Mountain Forests

Mountain forests contain many different kinds of trees and flowering shrubs. Slopes facing the sun are hot and dry. They provide very different growing conditions from shaded slopes. Some wildflowers need dense shade and shelter, while others prefer the open, dry forest floor.

As you climb a mountain, watch for the same flower in different stages of development. At lower elevations, the flower may already have produced seeds. Higher up, its blossom may just be opening. And higher yet, it may be distinguished only by its leaves poking through the soil.

Streams whisper, birds call and sing, and animals abound in the forest. Listen for the creak of two trees rubbing against each other. Savor a delicious huckleberry. Watch for squirrels dashing up and down their tree homes.

Queen's Cup

other names: Bead Lily, Bride's Bonnet
height: 2 to 6 inches
season: May to July

A lovely, white, six-pointed star rises above three oval leaves. *Uniflora* means "one-flowered," referring to the fact that each plant produces just one flower. Ruffed grouse like to eat the blue berries that form in the fall.

Clintonia uniflora

Trillium

other names: Wake Robin, Birthroot
height: 4 to 24 inches
season: March to May

"Tri" in the name trillium means three, just as it does in the word triangle. This plant has three large green leaves, three white petals that turn pinkish with age, three sepals, three styles, and three reddish berries. Trillium has the common name wake robin because it blooms early in spring—about when the first robins arrive. Ants love the trillium's oil-rich seeds and help scatter them throughout the forest. If you pick the bloom from a trillium, the plant may die or not bloom again for years.

Trillium ovatum

Pipsissewa

other names: Prince's Pine, Wintergreen, Waxflower
height: 2 to 12 inches
season: June to August

Waxy, pink flowers with protruding, green ovaries decorate the fragile stems of this evergreen plant. Look for these flowers under evergreen trees. Pipsissewa are more abundant after a forest fire. The Indian word *pipisisikweu* means "it breaks into small pieces," referring to the medicinal use of the leaves to break up kidney stones.

Chimaphila umbellata

Oregon Grape

other names: Mahonia, Barberry,
Holly Grape
height: 4 to 8 inches
season: March to June

This is a very colorful plant. In springtime, bright yellow blossoms cluster on the stems. Each autumn, the shiny, green, hollylike leaves change to a deep red, and the berries turn purplish-blue. Indians and settlers prepared various parts of the plant for food, medicine, drink, and dye. Flathead Indians cleaned cuts and scrapes with a solution of Oregon grape. Kootenai Indians made a tea from it for a blood tonic. You can boil the shredded bark and make a bright yellow clothing dye. Or add sugar to the berries to make a yummy jelly.

Mahonia repens

Elegant Cat's Ear

other names: Star Tulip
height: 2 to 8 inches
season: May to June

Each petal looks like a soft, hairy cat's ear. A deep purple crescent colors the center of the three petals, and one grasslike leaf arches over the blossoms. Bighorn sheep graze on the seedpods, and bears like to dig and eat the underground tubers.

Calochortus elegans

Yellow Ladyslipper

other names: Venus-Slipper
height: 12 to 18 inches
season: May to June

A brilliant yellow lip petal forms a tiny ballet slipper complete with long, striped, purple petals ready to tie around a tiny lady's ankle. Bees are good at retrieving the nectar, but other insects get trapped inside by the curled lower lip. As the scientific name *calceolus* suggests, ladyslippers like calcium-rich soils such as limestone. This is a rare orchid in Montana. You're lucky to see one.

Cypripedium calceolus

Heartleaf Arnica

other name: Leopard's Bane
height: 4 to 24 inches
season: April to July

The lower pairs of leaves are shaped like hearts. The cheery, sunflower-like flower head reaches above the forest floor. Arnica is one of the few sunflower-like plants that can tolerate fairly dense shade. Arnica has many medicinal uses and helps relieve aches, sprains, and bruises.

Arnica cordifolia

Sticky Geranium

other name: Crane's Bill
height: 1 to 3 feet
season: May to August

Bears, moose, elk, and deer like to eat these flowers and leaves. In late summer, it's easy to see how a geranium got its name. *Geranium* comes from the Greek word for "crane," and the fruit looks like the beak of a crane. If a fruit pod is ripe and still closed, touch it gently and watch the tiny cups fling seeds through the air.

Geranium viscosissimum

Indian Pipe

other names: Ghost Plant, Ice Plant, Corpse Plant
height: 2 to 12 inches
season: June to August

This waxy, translucent-white flower droops atop a thick stalk. It resembles an Indian peace pipe. Sometimes it turns light pink after it's fertilized. Indian pipe turns black where you touch it or as it gets old. A fungus growing on the roots helps Indian pipe steal nutrients from neighboring green plants.

Monotropa uniflora

Monkshood

other names: Friar's Cap,
Blue Weed
height: 1 to 7 feet
season: June to August

The upper sepal of the violet-blue flower forms an arching hood, like the hood of a monk's habit. Peek under the hood to find the monk's "face," composed of two petals and the stamen and pistil. We get heart medicine from some species of monkshood. Early Greek and Roman warriors used the plant juice to poison their arrows. A European relative of the monkshood is the famous "wolfbane" used to ward off werewolves. Yikes!

Aconitum columbianum

Golden Columbine

other name: Columbine
height: 1 to 3 feet
season: July to August

Hummingbirds use their long beaks to sample the nectar of columbines, but short, stubby bumblebees must drill holes in the spurs to get at the sweet prize. Columbine comes from the Latin word *columba,* meaning "dove." Can you see the five doves with their shared wings outspread?

Aquilegia flavescens

Clematis

other names: Virgin's Bower,
Traveler's Joy
height: vine climbs to 10 feet
season: May to July

Clematis vines love to climb. Twining shoots wind around a shrub or crawl along the ground, and the pretty, delicate, lilac-colored clematis blossoms droop gracefully from the vine. Each seed is adorned with a feathery, silver plume to help it fly in the wind.

Clematis columbiana

Mountain Meadows

Mountain meadows lie under snow much of the winter, are awash with snowmelt and rain in the spring and early summer, and often dry out completely in late summer and autumn. Flowers must be able to blossom and produce seeds quickly and then wait patiently until the next spring warms their home before they can grow again.

Indian Paintbrush

other name: Paintbrush
height: 10 to 30 inches
season: May to July

Look for the narrow, pale-green flowers hidden among the brightly colored bracts. The bracts, which look a bit like petals, range in color from magenta to yellow to orange to crimson. The roots of a paintbrush can burrow into the roots of a different plant, such as a sagebrush, and steal part of its food. Because of that ability, paintbrush is called a root parasite.

Castilleja spp.

Bottlebrush

other names: American Bistort, Snakeweed
height: 8 to 28 inches
season: May to August

From a distance, a bottlebrush blossom looks like a white clump of fuzz caught on the grass. Grizzlies and black bears dig and eat the stout root, and deer and elk graze on the leaves. Early Indians added the root to soups and stews.

Polygonum bistortoides

Monument Plant

other names: Green Gentian
height: 2 to 5 feet
season: June to August

Like a monument or statue in a grassy city park, the monument plant stands straight and erect above the surrounding meadow plants. Its long leaves are shaped like deers' tongues. Inconspicuous greenish-yellow flowers spring from the axils of the upper leaves. Look closely and notice the subtle beauty of each freckled blossom.

Frasera speciosa

Spring Beauty

other name: Groundnut
height: 2 to 10 inches
season: April to July

Look closely to see the thin, pink lines and yellow spot decorating the flower. Each of the five petals is notched at the top. Indians ate the nutty-tasting corm, a thick underground stem base. Black bears, grizzlies, and gophers dig and eat the corms in springtime. Elk, moose, deer, and sheep eat the leaves.

Claytonia lanceolata

Wallflower

other name: none
height: 1 to 3 feet
season: May to August

In Europe, this plant often grows in the rocky soil along old walls. Hence the name wallflower. In Montana you're more likely to see it in flat, open areas and on hillsides, from the lowest valleys to about 7,500 feet. The blossoms may be bright yellow, orange, or a dark burnt-orange color. Pikas, marmots, and bighorn sheep feast on the leaves and stems.

Erysimum capitatum

Bitterroot

other names: none
height: ½ to 2 inches
season: May to July

Bitterroot is the state flower of Montana. It was a very important root crop for Montana's Indians, and they taught Lewis and Clark to eat it. This is one of the few plants whose flowers open up about the same time the leaves shrivel up and disappear. The Flathead Indians tell a story about an old woman who cried bitter tears as her family was starving to death. A spirit bird took pity on her and sent the nourishing bitterroot to grow where each of her tears fell.

Lewisia rediviva

Shooting Star	Mountain Bluebell	Pussytoes

Shooting Star

other name: Bird's Bill
height: 6 to 16 inches
season: April to July

Perhaps one really windy day these fragrant flowers turned inside out and decided to stay that way. Now they appear to shoot through the sky like small, pink stars aimed at the earth. There are about ten species of shooting stars in the West. Flower color ranges from white to pink to deep purple. Native Americans roasted and ate the roots and leaves.

Dodecatheon pulchellum

Mountain Bluebell

other name: Bluebell, Chiming Bell
height: 1 to 4 feet
season: May to August

Little blue or pinkish tubular bells droop in clusters at the end of the stems. Bears, elk, deer, bighorn sheep, and marmots love to graze on this plant, and elk babies can hide under the tall foliage. Cute little pikas cut bluebell plants, let them dry in the sun, and then feed on the dried bluebell "hay" during the long, cold mountain winters.

Mertensia ciliata

Pussytoes

other names: Rose Pussytoes
height: 2 to 12 inches
season: May to August

Like furry little toes on a kitten, pussytoes invite you to touch them gently. The tiny flowers are hidden within the pinkish-red, furry "toes," or bracts. Painted Lady butterflies often lay their eggs on the undersides of the leaves. The feathery seed of the pussytoes reminds some people of a butterfly's antenna; hence the scientific name *antennaria*.

Antennaria microphylla

Bear Grass

other names: Indian Basket Grass, Squaw Grass, Elk Grass, Bear Lily
height: 2 to 5 feet
season: June to September

This plant is so popular that it's amazing any are left. Elk eat the flowers, stalks, and seedpods. Mountain goats eat bear grass in winter. Indians bleached the leaves and used them to weave clothing and baskets. And florists use the leaves in flower arrangements.

Xerophyllum tenax

Elephant Head

other name: Little Pink Elephant
height: 6 to 30 inches
season: June to August

If you examine the flower stalk closely, you'll see how this plant got its name. With its "trunk" raised as if trumpeting and earlike petals to either side, the flower only needs eyes to resemble a real pink elephant. The blossoms cluster close together around the stalk. Elk think this is a tasty treat in early summer.

Pedicularis groenlandica

Glacier Lily

other names: Dogtooth Violet, Trout Lily, Adder's Tongue
height: 6 to 10 inches
season: March to August

This beautiful, yellow lily loves really cold, wet places such as the edges of glaciers or snowfields. Every part of the plant is edible: Indians boiled and ate the bulbs and beanlike seedpods and nibbled the leaves and flowers for fresh salad greens. Glacier lilies are also eaten by mountain-dwelling animals such as bears, elk, bighorn sheep, mountain goats, and deer.

Erythronium grandiflorum

Streambanks and Wetlands

Sploosh! Splash! You might have to get your feet wet to see the flowers that grow here. Flowing water and muddy banks provide abundant moisture for many brightly colored flowers that grow along rivers and streams. These flowers live in the company of trout and beavers and brighten the way for many animals that come to the water to drink.

Marsh Marigold

other name: Elk's Lip
height: 1 to 8 inches
season: May to August

This water-loving plant is found near melting snowbanks or next to streams and lakes. The stems and undersides of the shiny leaves are tinged with purple. The pretty, white blossom has no petals, but its five to twelve sepals look like petals radiating around the bright yellow anthers. Elk love to eat marsh marigolds.

Caltha leptosepala

Monkeyflower

other name: Lewis' Monkeyflower
height: 1 to 3 feet
season: May to August

Why is it called monkeyflower? The Latin name *mimulus* means "mimic." And you know how monkeys like to copy, or mimic, things. Hummingbirds and sphinx moths are attracted to the pink, rose, or red flowers. Look closely to see little freckles on the lower petal. Monkeyflowers grow in clusters, usually near streams. If the plant falls over, roots will develop where the stem touches the soil. Native Americans and early settlers ate the plant raw and cooked.

Mimulus lewisii

Horsemint

other names: Nettleleaf Horsemint, Giant Hyssop
height: 1 to 5 feet
season: June to August

A dense spike of purple, lavender, or white flowers juts above the nettlelike leaves. This is the most important mint forage plant in the Rocky Mountains. Wild and domestic animals eat it, and birds like the seeds.

Agastache urticifolia

False Hellebore

other name: Corn Lily
height: 4 to 6 feet
season: June to August

From a distance, the tall stalk and deeply veined leaves of this plant make it look like garden corn. But don't sample any! False hellebore is so poisonous it can kill honeybees.

Veratrum californicum

Cattail

other name: none
height: 4 to 8 feet
season: June to November

Ever had a cattail pancake? Indians used every part of this plant: the pollen makes a flour for pancakes, breads, or cakes. The leaves can be woven into baskets. The downy seeds are good insulation and make good pillow stuffing or absorbent padding for diapers. And the roots are edible. The young flower heads can be boiled and eaten like corn on the cob. Many waterfowl and other birds like to nest among cattails.

Typha latifolia

Skunk Cabbage

other name: Yellow Arum
height: 1 to 2 feet
season: April to July

The poisonous leaf covering, called a spathe, smells a bit skunky when injured. The smell attracts pollinators like beetles, who like stinky, rotting things. Little ridges on the roots contract and pull the plant close to the ground each spring to keep the leaves and flower buds away from cold winds. The unusual knob of flowers is called a spadix.

Lysichitum americanum

Prairies and Grasslands

Prairie wildflowers must survive high winds, hot sun, and long periods with no rain. Many have evolved a very short life cycle and can grow, blossom, and produce seeds in just a few weeks. Some prairie plants have a waxy or hairy surface, which helps them preserve precious moisture. Others only open their blossoms in the cooler evenings or early mornings.

Montana's prairies include open plains, rugged breaks and coulees, and rolling hills. The prairie vegetation that Lewis and Clark found nearly 200 years ago was very different from what you can find today. Almost all the Montana prairie has either been plowed into cropland or grazed by livestock. Look for prairie wildflowers in cemeteries, along railroad tracks and country roads, and in unused fields.

While scouting for prairie wildflowers, listen for the song of a meadowlark, look for the flickering colors of butterflies, and watch the playful prairie dogs.

Prairie Rose

other name: Wild Rose
height: 6 to 18 inches
season: June to August

Rose bushes provide food and cover for such wildlife as pheasants, grouse, quail, and black bears. Humans like the "rosehips," a small fruit that may be pink, scarlet, or reddish-orange. Rosehips are so high in vitamin C that we use them to make vitamin tablets.

Rosa arkansana

Pasqueflower

other name: Prairie Crocus
height: 2 to 10 inches
season: April to May

These early blossoms open even before the leaves have pushed out of the ground. This flower blooms around Passover in mild climates, so we call it the French word for Passover: *pasque*. One Indian tribe called this plant "ears of the earth." The long, silver hairs of the seed head make it look like a furry little creature with hair in its eyes.

Anemone nuttalliana

Yellow Bell

other name: Yellow Fritillary
height: 3 to 8 inches
season: March to June

Bears, deer, pocket gophers, and ground squirrels like to dig and eat the corms of yellow bells. People can eat them, too. The raw corm tastes like a potato, and cooked corms taste more like rice. The shy, drooping, yellow, bell-shaped flower fades to a purplish color with age.

Fritillaria pudica

Dotted Gayfeather

other names: Blazing Star, Button Snakeroot
height: 2 to 10 inches
season: July to September

Gayfeathers look like lavender exclamation points in a late-summer meadow. As many as one hundred individual flowers cluster on each stiff, hairy stem. They bloom from the tip of the stem down. Feathery, purplish styles stick gaily out of each flower, and little glands dot the leaves. The roots of one plant can grow sixteen feet into the ground.

Liatris punctata

Prairie Coneflower

other name: Coneflower
height: 1 to 4 feet
season: July to September

This flower is best appreciated through a magnifying glass. The long, slender cone is covered with tiny, brown, tubular disk flowers—more than you can count. A few scraggly, yellow or purple ray flowers stick out of the bottom of the cone. Indians made tea from the flowers and leaves or boiled the flower heads to make a rust-colored clothing dye.

Ratibida columnifera

Blue Flax

other names: Prairie Flax
height: 8 to 24 inches
season: June to August

Fragile, blue petals often blow away in the afternoon breeze, but new blossoms open the next morning. Flax stems contain very useful fibers. The Egyptians wrapped their mummies in cloth of flax. Indians made ropes and fishing lines. We make linen thread and cloth from a cultivated flax. And flaxseed oil, also known as linseed oil, is an important part of some medicines, paints, varnishes, linoleums, and inks.

Linum perenne var. *lewisii*

Wild Iris

other name: Blue Flag
height: 8 to 20 inches
season: May to June

Iris was the Greek goddess of the rainbow. A rainbow of colors appears in the center of these blossoms. In some countries, the three petals symbolized faith, wisdom, and courage, so an iris was often carved into the top of a queen's or king's scepter. American Indians twisted the silky leaf fibers into twine and rope for fishing and hunting.

Iris missouriensis

Yarrow

other name: Milfoil
height: 1 to 3 feet
season: May to September

Yarrow is very aromatic and has many medicinal uses. The scientific name *achillea* was chosen because the famous Greek hero Achilles used yarrow to treat his wounded soldiers. Properly prepared, yarrow can help stop bleeding, increase perspiration and break a fever, and ease a rash.

Achillea millifolium

Wyoming Kittentail

other name: Wyoming Besseya
height: 3 to 10 inches
season: April to June

This furry little plant seems to invite a gentle touch, like petting a tiny kitten. It's easy to see the protruding stamen of each floret packed into the flower head. But don't look for petals—there aren't any. Kittentail's hairy leaves sometimes have red edges.

Besseya wyomingensis

Prickly Pear

other name: Plains Cactus
height: 3 to 6 inches, in clumps spreading as wide as 10 feet
season: May to July

Sioux and Crow Indians rubbed peeled prickly pears over newly painted hides to keep the colors fresh. The tasty, burgundy-colored "pear" fruit is enjoyed by both humans and animals. Be sure to peel off the prickly spines before eating the fruit.

Opuntia polyacantha

Steer's Head

other name: none
height: 2 to 4 inches
season: April to May

Two inner petals form a long nose, while the two outer petals curve upward like the horns on a miniature steer's head. This tiny, low-growing flower blooms early in spring among the sagebrush. Although it looks like a cow's head, steers and other livestock must avoid eating this poisonous plant.

Dicentra uniflora

Pincushion Cactus

other name: Nipple Cactus
height: 1 to 2 inches
season: May to June

This small, round cactus is often nearly buried in the ground. But beautiful, greenish-yellow flowers poke up toward the sunshine, and the plant produces a sweet, edible fruit in late summer. This cactus bristles with spines like a pincushion full of needles.

Coryphantha missouriensis

Arrowleaf Balsamroot

other name: Bigroot
height: 8 to 24 inches
season: April to July

This abundant flower has many uses. Its beautiful, sunflower-like flower heads brighten dry slopes around the state. Elk and deer munch on the young shoots, and bighorn sheep eat the flowers and leaves. Many Indian tribes knew medicinal uses of the plant, such as treating burns with a poultice made from the arrow-shaped leaves. They also peeled the young flower stems and ate them like we eat celery. Or they roasted the seeds and the big, woody roots. The cooked roots taste a bit like balsam.

Balsamorhiza sagittata

Camas

other names: Camash, Swamp Sego
height: 12 to 20 inches
season: April to June

Chamas is an Indian word meaning "sweet." Indians throughout the Northwest depended upon this nourishing plant and collected the sweet-tasting bulbs each autumn. They baked the bulbs and ground them into flour to make flat cakes. Camas was once so abundant in western Montana that a field of blooming camas looked like a lake of blue. Moose, elk, and deer graze on camas in springtime.

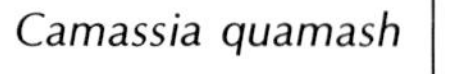

Camassia quamash

Evening Primrose

other names: Rock Rose, Sand Lily, Gumbo Primrose
height: 2 to 6 inches
season: May to July

The fragile, white blossoms unfold in the evening to await pollination by night-flying insects. The blossoms turn pink or red and then wilt when the sun shines on them the next morning. White-tailed deer, birds, and little rodents like to gobble the seeds.

Oenothera caespitosa

Prairie Smoke

other names: Long-Plumed Avens,
Old Man's Whiskers
height: 6 to 24 inches
season: May to July

Triflorum in the scientific name means "three-flowered." You'll find three flowers at the end of each stem. The inconspicuous, dark pink flowers hang like bells until they are fertilized. Then they turn upward, and feathery plumes grow straight up—like a punk hairstyle. The plumes help the seeds sail across the meadow to a new home. Some people think the white plumes look like tiny puffs of smoke on the prairie.

Geum triflorum

Lupine

other names: Bluebonnet,
Wolfbean
height: 1 to 2 feet
season: June to August

The word *lupus* is Latin for "wolf." People once thought lupine gobbled up nutrients in the soil. But today we know that lupine actually enriches the soil it inhabits. Lupine is still a good name for this plant, because we've also learned that wolves are a positive part of our natural world.

Lupinus spp.

Blanketflower

other name: Brown-Eyed Susan
height: 8 to 30 inches
season: June to August

This vivid flower can blanket a field in showy colors. Look closely at the blossom, called a composite. The brightly colored pinwheel parts are called ray flowers, and the center disk is composed of dozens of tightly packed, individual florets.

Gaillardia aristata

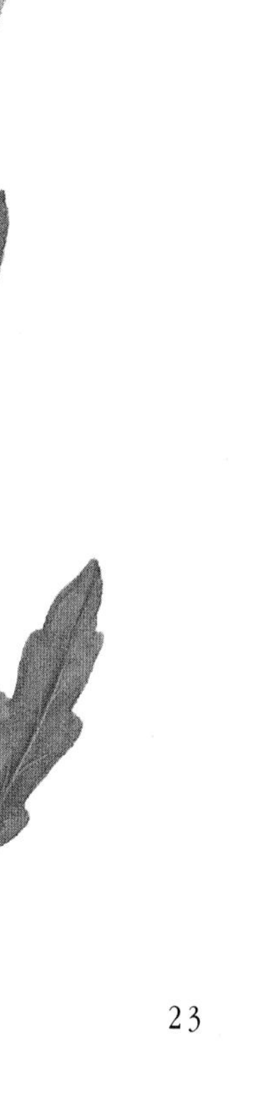

Roadside and Disturbed Areas

People have a way of disrupting natural plant communities. We bulldoze roads, dig ditches, build railroads, and make trails. We build homes and plant garden flowers that go to seed and sprout somewhere else. Sometimes fires, manmade or natural, burn an area, or a flooding river rushes through.

All these disturbances create unique conditions that many plants find too harsh. But some plants, often thought of as weeds, are able to grow and flourish. Some become a real nuisance. But others are an important part of nature because they stabilize the soil with their roots, add needed nutrients, and prepare the way for grasses, shrubs, and trees to grow in the disturbed area again someday.

Fireweed

other names: Willow Herb, Blooming Sally
height: 1 to 5 feet
season: June to September

Fireweed is often the first plant to grow after a forest fire. It helps enrich the burned area so that other plants can grow there again. Fireweed blooms from the bottom up, so you may see seedpods, flowers, and buds on one plant. Little parachute-like hairs on the seeds can carry them long distances.

Epilobium angustifolium

Butter and Eggs

other names: Toadflax
height: 1 to 2 feet
season: June to July

The blossom is gold and yellow, like an egg yolk in a pan of butter. The other common name is toadflax. Squeeze a blossom gently from the sides and watch it open like a toad's mouth. The juice from the leaves may stop the itch of your mosquito bites. Each plant can produce up to 250,000 seeds!

Linaria vulgaris

Knapweed

other names: Spotted Knapweed, Spotted Star-Thistle
height: 1 to 3 feet
season: June to September

Honeybees love the spiny, thistlelike, pinkish-purple flower bracts of knapweed. A single plant can produce a thousand seeds, and here in Montana it crowds out all neighboring vegetation. This Eurasian plant has become a real problem.

Centaurea maculosa

Wavyleaf Thistle

other name: Thistle
height: 1 to 6 feet
season: June to August

The roots of one wavyleaf thistle plant may spread out ten feet in every direction. Elk and bears eat the plant, although the sharp prickles discourage most other browsers. A legend tells why a thistle is the national emblem of Scotland. One night long ago, the Danes invaded Scotland and took off their boots to sneak up on a village. A soldier stepped on a thistle and yelled in pain, and the villagers awoke in time to defend themselves and their country.

Cirsium undulatum

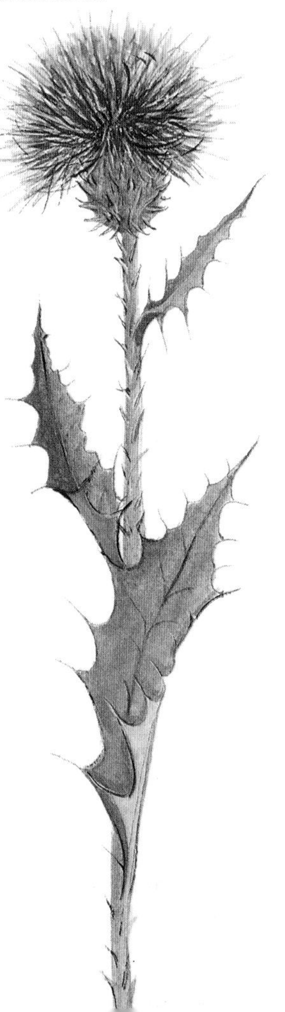

Salsify

other names: Oyster Plant
Goatsbeard
height: 16 to 32 inches
season: May to September

The yellow ray flowers produce a delicate, globe-shaped seed head, like a giant dandelion. Each seed has a tiny umbrella attached, to help the seed float far away on the wind. Look carefully—perhaps a really strong wind turned each little umbrella inside out. The nutritious taproot can be boiled and tastes a bit like oysters.

Tragopogon pratensis

Mullein

other names: Flannel Plant, Woolly Mullein, Miner's Candle
height: 2 to 7 feet
season: June to August

The word mullein comes from *moleyne,* an old English word for "soft." Hummingbirds line their little nests with soft hairs from the leaves. In olden times, the tall flower spike was dipped in tallow and burned as a torch for celebrations. It's fun to throw a dried stalk like a javelin.

Verbascum thapsus

Berries

Many plants produce berries after their flowers are fertilized. Some berries are delicious, while others are poisonous. Never eat a berry unless you know it's safe!

The soft pulp of a berry provides protection and nourishment for the seed enclosed within. Birds and animals eat the berries, helping to spread the plant to new sites. They also eat the leaves, stems, and even roots. People use many parts of berry plants for food, medicines, and dyes. No wonder so many berry bushes have thorns! They need some protection against overuse.

Strawberry

other name: none
height: 3 to 6 inches
season: April to June for blossoms, June to July for berries

Don't forget where you see the pretty, white, five-petaled blossoms, so you can return later to savor the sweet wild strawberries. Yum! Birds, turtles, small rodents, and bears also enjoy eating them. This plant got its name because many people lay straw under their garden strawberries to keep them from rotting on wet ground.

Fragaria virginiana

Thimbleberry

other name: Salmonberry
height: 3 to 5 feet
season: May to June for blossoms, June to July for berries

Thimbleberry bushes don't stick you with prickly stems when you sample the berries. Gently pull a berry off the bush and see how it fits over the end of your finger like a sewing thimble. Bears love to eat the salmon-pink or whitish berries, and deer nibble the leaves. Thimbleberries often form thickets nearly impossible to walk through.

Rubus parviflorus

Huckleberry

other name: none
height: 6 to 24 inches
season: June to July for blossoms, July to August for berries

Many people think huckleberries are the most flavorful berries in the world. Animals think so, too. Huckleberries are a staple food for black bears. Grouse, ptarmigans, rodents, martens, coyotes, and many other birds and mammals eat them, too.

Vaccinium globulare

Wild Currant

other names: Wax Currant
height: 3 to 10 feet
season: April to June for blossoms, August to September for berries

Many Indian tribes dried these currants and then added them to dried meat and fat to make pemmican, a nutritious traveling food. Today, people often mix the currants with sugar and make jelly. Bears, rodents, and many birds seek out these tart treats. Deer and elk browse the green leaves.

Ribes cereum

Kinnikinnick

other names: Bearberry, Manzanita
height: 3 to 6 inches
season: May to June for blossoms, July to August for berries

Kinnikinnick is an Algonquin Indian word for "mixed." Indians mixed the leaves with other plants to make pipe tobacco. When cooked slowly, the bland berries pop like popcorn. Deer and bighorn sheep browse on the evergreen leaves and twigs in winter, and songbirds, turkeys, grouse, rodents, and bears eat the berries.

Arctostaphylos uva-ursi

Chokecherry

other names: none
height: to 20 feet
season: May to June for blossoms, August to September for fruit

Chokecherries are really tart, and hard to "choke" down raw. But you can make excellent pies, syrups, jams, and jellies from the fruit. A light frost usually makes the chokecherry a little bit sweeter. Indians dried the berries and ate them throughout the winter in their pemmican and stew. Chokecherry leaves are poisonous but the bark has strong medicinal qualities, especially good in treating stomach problems.

Prunus virginiana

Conclusion

"Over here! Look at me!" shout the bright colors of a wildflower. The showy blossom attracts us, but more importantly, it attracts insects and other flying and crawling visitors that pollinate each flower. Bees, moths, beetles, butterflies, hummingbirds, and even ants and bats are essential for the wildflowers to make seeds.

All of nature is interconnected. We humans are as dependent upon clean air and water as is the tiniest wildflower. Next time you stoop down to inhale the sweet smell of a fresh blossom, remember that we, too, unblossom and unfold in the natural world. Learn all you can and treat it gently—the earth is our most precious treasure.

Glossary

Alternate	Not opposite each other
Annual	A plant that lives for one season
Anther	The part of the stamen containing pollen
Basal	Near the base, at the bottom
Berry	Fleshy fruit containing seeds
Biennial	A plant that lives for two years, blooming only the second year
Bract	Leaflike scale
Bulb	A plant storage organ, usually below the ground
Corm	Bulblike underground swelling of a stem
Composite	Flower head composed of a cluster of ray and disk flowers
Disk flower	Tubular floret in the center part of a composite flower head
Evergreen	Bearing green leaves throughout the year
Filament	The stalk of the stamen
Floret	A small flower that is part of a cluster
Flower	Part of a plant containing male and/or female reproductive parts
Flower head	A dense cluster of flowers atop a stem
Fruit	Seed-bearing part of a plant; ripened ovary
Habitat	The place where a plant naturally grows and lives
Head	A dense cluster of flowers atop a stem
Herb	A plant with no woody stem above ground
Irregular	Not symmetrical in shape
Nectar	Sweet liquid produced by flowers to attract insects
Opposite	A pair of leaves opposite each other on a stem
Ovary	Part of the pistil that contains the developing seeds
Parasitic	Growing on and deriving nourishment from another plant

Pathfinders	Lines on a plant that guide insects to the nectar
Pedicel	Supporting stem of a single flower
Perennial	A plant that lives from year to year
Petals	Floral leaves inside the sepals that attract pollinators
Petiole	The stem supporting a leaf
Pistil	Seed-bearing organ of a flower
Pollen	Powderlike cells produced by stamens
Ray flowers	The flowers around the edge of a flower head; each flower may resemble a single petal
Regular	Alike in size and shape
Rhizome	Underground stem or rootstock
Saprophyte	A plant that lives on dead organic matter
Seed	Developed female egg
Seedpod	Sac enclosing the developed female egg(s)
Sepal	Outermost floral leaf that protects the delicate petals
Shrub	Low woody plant, usually having several stems
Spadix	Fleshy spike that bears flowers
Spathe	Leafy covering connected to the base of a spadix
Spur	Hollow appendage of a petal or sepal
Stamen	Pollen-producing organ of a flower
Stigma	The end of the pistil that collects pollen
Style	The slender stalk of a pistil
Succulent	Pulpy, soft, and juicy
Tendril	Slender, twining extension of a leaf or stem
Tuber	Thickened underground stem having numerous buds
Whorl	Three or more leaves or branches growing from a common point

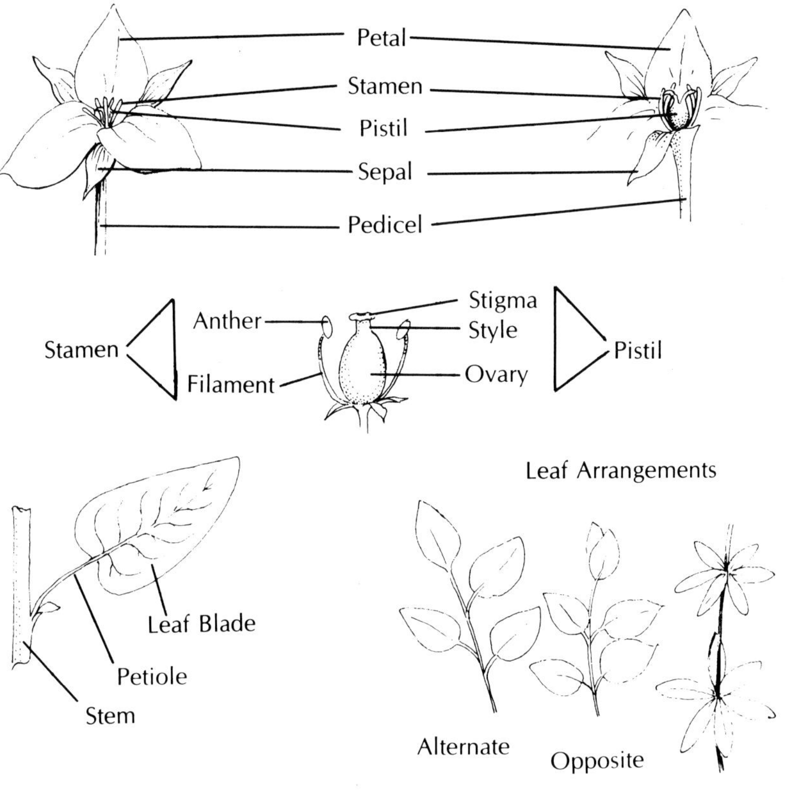

Where to See Wildflowers

Wildflowers can be found almost anywhere in Montana, but some of the best places are parks, forests, nature centers, and recreation areas. Many of these areas have campgrounds, picnic areas, nature trails, and interpretive services to help visitors see and appreciate these lands and their wildflowers. You can get information by contacting the following organizations:

State Parks and Wildlife Management Areas
Montana Department of Fish, Wildlife, and Parks
1420 East Sixth Avenue
Helena, MT 59620
(406) 444-2535

National Forests
USDA Forest Service, Northern Region
Federal Building
P.O. Box 7669
Missoula, MT 59807
(406) 329-3511

Bureau of Land Management
222 North 32nd Street
Box 36800
Billings, MT 59107
(406) 255-2885

Glacier National Park
West Glacier, MT 59936
(406) 888-5441

Yellowstone National Park
P.O. Box 168
Yellowstone National Park, Wyoming 82190
(307) 344-7381

The Nature Conservancy
P.O. Box 258
Helena, MT 59624
(406) 443-0303

National Wildlife Refuges
Department of the Interior
U.S. Fish and Wildlife Service
Box 25486
Denver Federal Center
Denver, CO 80225
(303) 236-7904

Where you can see wildflowers in Montana cities:

Billings—Along the Yellowstone River
Bozeman—Montana State University Arboretum, Kirk Hill Nature Area
Great Falls—Along the Missouri River
Helena—Mount Helena
Kalispell—Along the Flathead River
Missoula—Rattlesnake Park